Re-Humanize

Re-Humanize

Marlee Liss

The Awakened Press

The Awakened Press
www.theawakenedpress.com

For information about special discounts or for bulk purchases, please
contact The Awakened Press at books@theawakenedpress.com.

The Awakened Press can bring authors to your live event. For more
information or to book an event contact books@theawakenedpress.com or
visit our website at www.theawakenedpress.com.

Cover design by Henry Power Jokela
Original Cover Art and Illustrations by Marielle Rosky
Cover and Interior Design by David Moratto

The resources provided are accurate at the time of publication.

Printed in the United States of America.
Second The Awakened Press trade paperback edition.

ISBN: 979-8-9860377-0-7

Praise for Marlee's Story and Advocacy

"I picked up this book and couldn't put it down. It is raw and honest and written by one of the bravest souls. It comes at a time when we all need to be brave and especially supportive of one another. This book and this author lead that charge."

—Maureen

"This book is what the best poetry and soulful writing are made of... humility and authenticity. I'm in love with it. The perfect medicine for our wounded hearts."

—Danielle Dulsky, author

"Soul touching book. It gives a very strong message in a beautiful way. Highly recommend this book for everybody. It's very educational. The author has one brave spirit that transformed trauma into art and teachings."

—Rocio Campo

"The book is an incredibly deep look into Marlee's journey. It teaches everyone the importance and value in emotions and everyone who reads It will take something from It. Marlee is truly an exceptional human being."

—Arlene Sager

"I cannot express how wonderful this book is. I have never experienced what the author has been through, however I was so moved by this book. I truly believe that this book can be used in a variety of situations and can be a great support and a mode a positive motivation. I also strongly believe that it should be part of our high school curriculum. Everyone should own a copy of this book."

—Alessandra

"I want you to know this helped my healing process, a tear dropped because well I have had a rough time in the past 6 years. Thanks you for walking in your truth and speaking about it. I am inspired and touched by your bravery. Thank you."
　　—Esther

"Your story has gone beyond textbooks and readings and has allowed me to realize the great potential for restorative justice on all parties involved. You have completely changed and shaped the way I think about justice. This impact did not just happen to me, as speaking to my peers, you and your story have had an enormous impact on shaping the ideas of justice on a broader scale. You are an inspiration and you have encouraged me to become an advocate for restorative justice."
　　—Ashton

"I will be forever thankful for hearing your story. It was the first time that the concept of restorative justice really made sense to me, and I hope to continue to adopt this approach for my own personal conflicts, integrate it into my professional and personal relationships, and teach it to the youth of tomorrow so that the justice system of the future is one we would barely recognize today, with a community-based network focused on inclusion, reintegration, and love."
　　—Daniel

"I was incredibly inspired by Marlee's courage and shared education around the need for alternative models of justice for sexual violence. I hired Marlee as guest presenter for our Crime, Gender, and Sex lecture hall twice over the course of two years. In both instances, Marlee delivered an insightful, educational and emotionally moving presentation on restorative justice, emphasizing why survivors may seek out and benefit from this justice model. Students received an in-depth look at restorative justice and learned about survivors needs after sexual violence."
　　—University of Toronto Professor

"Marlee really showed how the ability to truly empathize with others can be used as a strength, rather than a weakness... Thank you for teaching me that forgiveness can sometimes be the only closure that we need. Thank you for teaching me that it is possible to get past the hard times in life, no matter how impossible it may seem in the moment."

—Jeevan

"Thank you Marlee for teaching me lessons I simply could not learn in the classroom. One huge takeaway I got from listening to you speak, is that when something terrible happens to you, you owe it to yourself to engage in meaningful, long-lasting healing. Thank you for showing me what justice really is, for pointing out the ways in which our criminal justice system is failing and the related things I want to change within myself. Above all thank you for being so brave. Without your courage I would still be in the dark, but you showed me the way out. You taught me lessons worth more than gold!"

—Brayden

I would like to acknowledge that I am speaking from an intersectional reality that includes both oppressed and privileged identities. My experiences have been shaped by my identity as a Jewish, lesbian woman and simultaneously, my perspective is limited by my privilege as a white, able-bodied and cisgendered person.

I also want to take a moment to offer a major Trigger Warning for this book. I share about my experience with sexual violence and an in-depth look at the healing that followed. To my fellow survivors: You are loved. Please be gentle with yourself as you read. Honour your limits, your pace and your sense of safety.

Lastly, I want to encourage you to research the evolution of my story at the completion of this book. I hope that the closure I found can inspire you, ignite hope, and raise awareness for alternative healing pathways. I am humbled and empowered to have made history in the justice system and to now dedicate my life to working with women and non-binary folk as a somatic coach, restorative justice advocate and award-winning speaker. Every day, I get to work with folks who are courageously reclaiming self-love and embodied empowerment. You can learn more about my story and work at www.marleeliss.com.

*For everyone who has been led to believe that
they are anything less than entirely whole.*

Contents

Prologue

HELLO BEAUTIFUL READER, I am so happy to be sharing this second edition of Re-Humanize with you. So much has blossomed, evolved, changed, and rearranged since the original release of this book in 2017.

Since this book's first release, I've taken journeys that have felt much like homecomings. Most importantly, that's included coming out as lesbian, reclaiming Jewish identity and roots, and finding restorative justice. I've lived through a global pandemic (like you!) and I have also launched a business entirely dedicated to supporting women and non-binary folk in sensual reclamation and healing. For this assault I wrote about in these pages, I journeyed through the criminal justice system for three years. I felt the painful patriarchal depths of the punitive system, learned about the realities of the prison system, and decided I didn't believe in this dehumanizing form of "justice". Upon researching alternatives to the punitive system, I came across restorative justice, which prioritizes repair over punishment. I surrounded myself with supports, both emotional and legal, and began fighting for this outcome. After much back and forth, drama, prayer, hopelessness, faith, and tension—my sexual assault case became the first in North America to conclude with restorative justice through the courts.

My restorative justice outcome means that the man who raped me went to therapy, rather than proceeding to criminal trial. Eventually, we met in an eight-hour circle, which included myself, my assailant and his friend, my lawyer, a crown attorney, my mom and my sister sharing as people impacted by this assault. We gathered to process grief, create space for humanity, give voice to pain, create transformation, experience accountability, and actively break cycles of harm. I like to say that the circle was beyond my expectations, but aligned with my dreams. It was empowering, intense, difficult, liberating, and healing beyond what I thought was possible.

Since then, I have so far shared my story in *Buzzfeed, Forbes, Huff Post, Canadian Jewish News, CTV News, Walrus Magazine* and on the *Mel Robbins Show.* As an award-winning speaker, I've delivered keynotes at Fordham School of Law, University of Toronto, and Canadian Restorative Justice Symposium. I was honoured to be 1 of 25 survivors across Canada sitting on an elite panel to inform the National Action Plan to End Gender-Based Violence and to deliver presentations for US Military SAPRO, One Standard of Justice and the nation's Victims and Survivors of Crime Week.

I am eternally grateful to the Indigenous, Jewish, and Mennonite communities who created these principles and practices of restorative justice, as well as the Black and transgender communities who created transformative justice. I am eternally grateful to every individual who has opened their minds, ears, and hearts to my story, which reflects the wants, needs, actions, and hopes of so many of us. Restorative principles have changed my understanding of justice and shaped every area and interpersonal relationship in my life. For those role-modelling the ability to hold nuance, act upon faith in transformation and practice courageous love, I am grateful.

Upon sharing my story with the world, I received (and continue to receive) hundreds of thousands of messages from folks all over the world. I've heard from survivors, those who have caused harm, and all kinds of people impacted by sexual violence. In some moments, this made me feel held, empowered, lit up for this mission and so gorgeously far from being alone. In other moments, these messages felt devastating and heavy. I allowed all of these contrasting feels to move me into action, resulting in a life of dedication to restorative justice advocacy, professional speaking and somatic coaching.

As a coach, I draw from my background in anti-oppressive social work, trauma-informed yoga and somatic sex education. I have had the absolute pleasure of supporting hundreds of women and non-binary folk internationally in sensual reclamation. Supporting clients in feeling beautiful, safe and powerful in their bodies has been the most soul-nourishing work. Every session leaves my heart full, humbled, sparked and inspired. While healing is not linear or easily quantifiable, I have seen miraculous results; i.e., this has included individuals breaking silence on trauma, leaving toxic relationships, coming out as queer, setting long suppressed boundaries with family members, healing from body dysmorphia, feeling safe within their sexuality, pursuing their impact-driven dream career, creating trauma trainings for legal professionals, building apps to educate the public on consent culture, adopting a feminist sex-positive approach to parenting, and so much more. I want to thank every single one of my clients for being courageous in turning fully towards themselves despite everything in our culture that tells us to abandon our wants, desires, feelings, needs and centres.

We are all so worthy of this homecoming.

While the second edition of this book includes edits to the facilitated discussion pages, mainly reflecting gender inclusivity and my own queerness, the poems remain unchanged. At times, it is difficult for me to revisit the words that I wrote in the depths of such pain and trauma. However, I am so proud of the me who wrote this and chose to share it. This was perhaps the first time I allowed my raw, vulnerable, messy truth to be seen. These pages represent the process of questioning and waking up to rape culture for the very first time. It's the imperfect unpacking of so much of the patriarchal, cis-heteronormative messaging we are being given. The words you'll read in this book are also evidence of just how brilliant our bodies, spirit and survival mechanisms are. In moments where I could not speak or feel safe enough to be present in my body, I reached for my pen. Like humans have been doing for centuries, I took my heartbreak and made it into art. In doing so, I found solace, deeper peace, presence and affirming connection.

Thank you for picking up this book, talking about the hard stuff and being willing to question much of what society has taught us. Thank you for your bravery in turning towards your feelings throughout this book, whatever they may be. Emotion is where our empathy lives and our world is in need of more empathy. Do your best to notice your body as you read, breathe deep into your belly and take breaks when these words feel too heavy. Dance parties, power ballads, bright colours and things that sparkle always help me lighten the load.

Remember, you're so much more than the worst thing you've ever done and the worst thing that's ever happened to you. You are worthy of love and in this very moment, so many people in this world are glad that you exist—myself included.

With gratitude and heart,
Marlee Liss

Visit www.marleeliss.com for healing resources, to learn more about my story of restorative justice after sexual violence or to inquire about my speaking engagements and/or coaching programs.

Introduction

THE DAY AFTER I was raped I picked up a pen and started writing. Journalling had been a lifetime practice of mine, but my thoughts were too jumbled to write full coherent entries. Instead, I wrote short excerpts. I wrote words that were so destructive in my head and yet so creative on paper. And the outcome was this book, which is synonymous with my survival. This project became my lifeline; it forced me to learn, it allowed me to communicate what I was going through with (some) family and friends and it helped me turn harmful thoughts into creations to be proud of.

Through this experience, I have realized how uncomfortable people are in discussing sexual assault and how rape is treated like a curse word. But this is a real problem and we cannot fix a problem without gaining compassion and understanding. A week after my trauma, in a brave moment, I shared a post on social media "outing" myself as a sexual assault victim. I wanted to spark conversation and challenge the idea that silence is the exception. I wanted to teach people how to hold space for trauma and to create a new narrative of an "Empowered Victim". The response was overwhelming — from those who wanted to support and from those who needed support. I realized quickly (with the help of numerous panic attacks) that it was unrealistic for me to jump from victim to activist in a week. So I combined my activism with my healing and I kept writing: a combination of poems and facilitated questions that I hoped would one day inspire change, compassion, human connection and collective healing.

Re-Humanize is a book for everyone. It is a collaboration between author and reader that offers interactive discussion questions and the sharing of my personal journey. It touches on various connecting issues including challenging rape culture, beauty constructs, eating disorders, depression, anxiety, PTSD and inspiring women's empowerment. It speaks to those who have experienced objectification, which has been used to justify violence and feelings of "not enough-ness". It is also meant for feminists and allies wishing to gain a deeper understanding of such experiences. And for survivors it is a gift: I hope that the sharing of my own journey will provide you with some solace and comfort in knowing that you are not alone. I hope my words will serve as a gentle reminder that your feelings are valid, that your survival alone makes you a warrior, that you are a gift to this world, worthy of reclaiming your voice, your body, and your soul.

End of August

I am a child once again.
Needing to be held.
Guided.
Soothed.
Needing a nightlight to offer refuge
From the darkness that lies behind my eyelids

And

I am older than I thought possible.
Weary.
Used and tainted
Like a thing that sits in an attic
Gathering dust and cobwebs
Becoming the kind of sad that is uncomfortable to look at
And is easier to cast aside

This is the paradox of rape survival.

The lack of sleep
Leaves me with a headache.
My head pulses
In the same rhythm as his thrusts
And regardless of where I am,
That is where I am.

I am usually the one who fills and
I am not quite sure how to survive as the one who drains

You cover my mouth after I cry out
And continue thrusting
You apologize in a voice that sounds sincere
As if you cannot control what your body is making you do
It would be easier to understand
If you did not apologize
If you did not have a heart at all

I need a plate to smash
A wall to hit
A glass to break
So that I do not break myself

I wonder what he is doing right now
I shudder to think he is just casually existing

There is moaning and
There is crying and
The distinction is important
He must know this distinction
He must learn it
And study it
So that he recognizes the sound before it is a sound at all

Lying down on my stomach
Takes me back to staring at your wall
Motionless
Aside from the shaking
As empty as the lifeless object you just made me into
You leave and come back with a towel
To wipe the cum off of my back
The cum that you sprayed all over me
Marking your territory
Your conquest

I keep staring at the wall
Unmoving
As you repeat the words
"So sorry"
Again and again

Exploring: Anger

"Anger is a cue that something is wrong; to help mobilize our psychological and physical resources in order to help one combat injustice and abuse."

— HENDRIE WEISINGER, PH.D.[1]

• *What messages have you been taught about anger? Consider that anger management is not called "anger elimination".*

• *Studies have found that anger actually lowers levels of cortisol (the stress hormone). What are some practices to embrace anger and to express it in a functional way? How might such practices help prevent harm towards the self and others?*

• *In what ways are women and non-binary folk specifically taught to inhibit the expression of anger?*

• *What messages have you received about anger in relation to femininity (i.e., unpack narratives like "anger is unattractive or unladylike")? Do you associate anger with masculinity?*

• *"A 2008 study found that both men and women gave less professional status to women who expressed anger, while men who showed anger were promoted."[2] Why do you think this is? In what ways do we sacrifice our own well-being and comfort in order to appear polite?*

You get up and pace around your apartment
Because the voice of your conscience is beginning to speak up
You say "This is so fucked" and
"I am so sorry"
At this point I could have ran but
My head was spinning and
My body frozen and
My muscles so tightly clenched that
I was struggling to breathe, let alone stand up
After some kind of predatory pep talk you come back and enter me
This time quicker
Harder—
Perhaps creating a whirlwind
Loud enough to drown out that voice of conscience
That exists somewhere in your head

My body responds by clenching
So tightly that
All my muscles shake
Part of me thinks that if I clench tight enough
Your penis won't fit at all and that would be the end of it
But you twist this fear response into
Something more suited to your needs and say
"It's so sexy when you play with your vagina like that"
And now the only resistance mechanism I had
Has become a way to feed your fire and
I realize,
I am helpless

"It's not your fault"
The nurse says.
And now I am five years old
And crying
And she is holding me

Like blood on a sidewalk
Or fingerprints on a gun
My body itself has become the evidence
"Don't shower" they say
All you have to bring to the hospital tomorrow is
Yourself—
Dried semen on your back
Saliva in your crotch
The scent of his sweat on your skin
And all

The loudest kind of victim blaming
Comes from the victim herself

— Tainted

All I can hear is his own moaning
As he fingers me
The sound of him
Spitting into my vagina
My body is on my side and it knows
Not to get wet for him
But he finds a way to produce his own water

I hate this soundtrack.

Sometimes I stare into space for so long
That I have to try and convince myself that
I am alive
I am Human

But I find this difficult to believe
Because I witnessed somebody convincing themselves
That I am not human
And now I am unsure if my existence is objective
After being reduced to a mere object
So I just keep staring
My insides as empty as the space that holds my gaze

Exploring: Objectification

Objectification means, "...viewing and/or treating a person as an object, devoid of thought or feeling. Often, objectification is targeted at women and reduces them to objects of sexual pleasure and gratification."[3]

- *What are some ways that objectification exists? What are some examples of women and non-binary folk in the media being portrayed as objects rather than humans?*

- *What is implied within this wording: "women give it up" and "men get some"? How does this language contribute to the commodification of women's bodies?*

- *How would you define self-objectification? Have you experienced self-objectification? What is the impact of this experience?*

- *How might these concepts contribute to appearance anxiety and eating disorders, as well as violence towards women and non-binary folk?*

- *How does our society profit from women and non-binary folk disliking their bodies? Discuss how self-love may pose a threat to profit-motivated companies.*

The trees are still beautiful
It is both comforting and sad

Happy one week of survival after rape
Congratulations on surviving
Sorry about the rest of it
Unfortunately if you want people to celebrate with you
They will have to descend into that black hole you're sitting in
Maybe they can just peer into it
Look down from the top
And try to make out the figure that is you at the bottom
To say:

Congratulations on surviving

September Begins

There is the Macro
The sisterhood
The activism
The strength
The uprising
The chance to be an alchemist
To take crap and transmute it into something beautiful
To create an army of impactful humans
To fight hate with infinite love

Then there is the Micro
The: me
The darkness
The punching walls
The hours of staring into space
The getting lost in space
The nausea when someone says "me too"
The running when someone brushes my arm on the street
The longing to be invisible when I catch a man's gaze
The fear of loud music
The tears after trying to use a tampon
The twitching in my muscles
The shaking in my arms
The emptiness

I keep them separate
To heal
To make change
To survive,
I do both
But I keep them separate

And then I try to breathe

I thought sex was objectively good
I thought rape would be like: *I hate that it feels good*
I thought it was a science
Touch this nerve, adrenaline pumps, endorphins release, good feelings
    are had

But I learned that this is wrong
And this is kind of beautiful
Because every act of sex then is an act of surrender
Of letting go and being present
Of allowing your feelings to take you on an adventure
To climax and back, while sharing the thrill of this journey with another

But it is also kind of foul
Because the exact motions that can create adventure
Can also feel like a tragedy, an earthquake, a tsunami
An explosion that is more like a bomb than an orgasm
Something that can be done to you without your participation
Or Consent

Maybe sex is neutral like power or fire
Capable of both creation and destruction

I am confused when the panic attacks happen
These hives are an anaphylactic reaction
This inability to hear is from music played too loud
This nausea is just the heat
What is happening in my body is not the cause of an emotion
Not the cause of fear
Not some expression of post-traumatic stress

It can't be.

Because my body is not connected to my mind at all
That link between what I think and what I feel
It was dissevered
When my body became someone else's

I observe them walking
But my legs are not my legs
I observe them moving
But my hands are not my hands
My body is not my body
It was taken

So perhaps this will all go away if I just play my music a little quieter
Call it dumb
Call it illogical
But rationality does not belong in this realm of absurd action

I am not brave
I am not a hero
I am not a "better" kind of survivor
I am doing what I need
To heal
Impact,
Taking a wound and turning it into a flower
Alchemy,
Transmuting pain into gold

Your "me too's" are compassionate
They show me the strength of my voice
Your "me too's" are nauseating
They make me stare at the ceiling in silence for hours

Maybe it is a mere selfish distraction
A way to bring the attention away from my own pain
I'm not sure if the intent really matters
In comparison to the outcome

But:
I want to stop silence
Silence is a monster
Rape is a monster

"I have a misplaced fear of the soccer team," I say laughing
And my friends nod and understand
It is a fear of power and masculinity
The kind that destroys and doesn't create
That dehumanizes and only calls at 3am
That has been taught to win
And to keep score of their conquests
To use language that asserts their dominance like
Did you hit that? Tap that? Did you bang? Get the kill?

It is strange how the language we use to describe sex is also the
     language we use to describe warfare
It is strange how one person could say *lovemaking* and another could
     say *fucking*
I have to assume that the person is simply as harsh as their words
And now I say it without laughing because I find it strange that I
     wasn't already scared of the soccer team

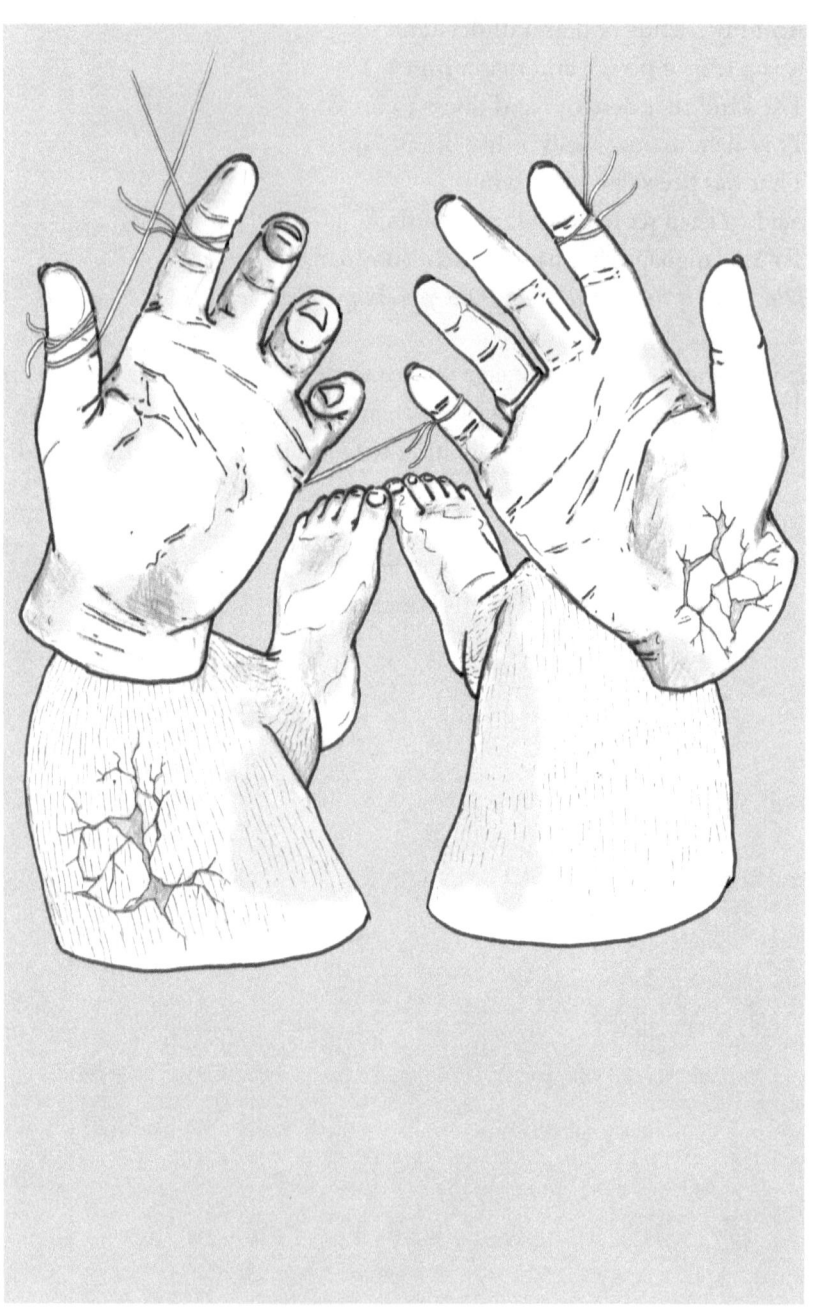

Exploring: Gender-Specific Groups

- *In what ways do groups of women and non-binary folk (often unintentionally) reinforce sexism? How does vocalizing insecurities encourage women and non-binary folk around us to internalize harmful messages? What feelings come up for you when a woman or non-binary person peer shames their own body or objectifies themselves?*

- *Studies show that athletes participate in approximately one third of sexual assaults on college campuses. What might be the cause of this correlation between sport and violence?*

- *What does toxic masculinity look like? How does this differ from healthy expressions of masculinity?*

- *It is damaging for a woman or non-binary person to "slut shame" another woman or non-binary person (known as lateral violence), just as it is damaging for a man to put another man on a pedestal for "getting girls".*

I am taking destruction
And making creation

I am taking rape
And making art

I am taking victimhood
And making sisterhood

—Alchemy

I say his name out loud in my session with her
It tastes bitter in my mouth
Like vomit
Like hate
Rising up my throat
Making me cringe
I shudder
And then swallow it down

"Step outside of your comfort zone"
I used to do that a lot
I flourished under a sense of possibility and challenge
I built a comfort zone as vast as a whole country
Its walls made from pride born out of demolished self-doubts
It was a place to run
To try
To fail
To live

But this haven built upon playful trial and error
It was invaded
With your weapons and your manhood

And now it is much too easy to step outside of my comfort zone
But this looks more like a push
A stumble forward, rather than a step
And the stumble comes with knots in my stomach
And panic in my chest

And it is nearly impossible
To step outside of this new discomfort zone
That is as vast as the whole world
There is no place of refuge from the whole world

I remember sitting on a field of flowers
Surrounded by majestic trees and blue skies
And feeling sad for those who have confined themselves
To a smaller playground that is made of plastic parts
I remember wanting to tell them that the playground was outside of
    that container
The real playground is made of earth
Not plastic

But now I sit with them
Hiding inside the playground
In its quietest corner
Wishing to remain unseen
Confined to an artificial container of safety
I am sad for those who are beside me
And I am scared for those who are outside, on the real playground
The trees, flowers and blue skies that I once worshipped as some
    infinite art gallery now look more like a ground for battle

Hiding in a shelter is not living
Walking frightfully across a war zone is not living

I lied in my previous poem
I denied that endorphins were released
When he stuck his fingers inside me
And said "but it still feels good right?"
And then came the moment I started hating myself
Because I didn't believe the No that came out of my own mouth

She made me acknowledge that scientifically, pleasure is involved in rape
Those words are nauseating:
Pleasure is involved in rape
That is why we feel gross
That is why we feel tainted
That is why we self-blame and become crushed under this voice in the
    back of our minds that says: Maybe some part of me wanted this

Fuck my nerves
And my ligaments
And the release of hormones at the moment of forced touch
Don't tell me I am not disgusting
Don't tell me it is normal to respond to an attack with a No that
    sounds like: please stop and please continue
Don't tell me that these are not mixed messages
Don't tell me that it is not my fault
I ignore my body entirely so that I don't have to face this twisted
    pleasure that was born alongside all of the pain

Exploring: Consent

"Most sensitive are the nerves in our sexual parts.
When these are stimulated, through thought or physical
sensation, nerves respond. Sexual responses are automatic.
A girl may suddenly find her nipples harden when stroked
by a rapist. High stress and anxiety themselves trigger
sexual responses. Abuse is abuse whether or not
you responded sexually."

— MALTZ [4]

• *How does a physical response differ from pleasure? How might sexual
assault survivors be psychologically impacted by this disconnect?*

• *How do you define consent? What are some ways to distinguish
between sexual response (i.e., physical arousal) vs. consent?
Why do you think people may lack understanding of consent?*

• *How can we weave practices of consent into our everyday interactions,
in and outside of intimate moments?*

• *Historically, how might men have been taught that they have
ownership of non-binary folks' and women's bodies?*

• *Take some time to unpack the comment, "But it still feels good, right?"
and how this interweaves with manipulation and non-consent.*

• *Why is it important to go beyond a "no means no" approach to consent
and to instead adopt a "yes means yes" approach? What is the difference?*

The Longest Month

I can choose to identify as an object
I can say I am a table
And assume that my being perceived as a table is inevitable
I can choose my actions accordingly
If I go on all fours
It is expected that someone will place more objects on top of me
As I am a table

Or I can choose to identify as a human
And so being on all fours does not necessarily mean someone will
    place objects on top of me like they would a table
They will likely refrain from doing so, as they see I have a face
And a heart
Like them

Similarly

I can identify as someone existing within rape culture
I can change my name to: Potential Victim
And I can assume that my being raped as Potential Victim is inevitable
I can choose my actions accordingly
I can wear high collar shirts
And drink less and use a buddy system
Because I assume that my being perceived as Potential Victim is inevitable
Because I am merely Potential Victim

Or I can choose to identify as a human
I can step outside of rape culture
And say that being drunk does not necessarily mean someone will
    rape me
Like they would Potential Victim
I can assume that they may refrain, as they see I have a face
And a heart
Like them

— My sister's response to her self-blaming sister

Self-Fulfilling Prophecy:

I became as still and lifeless
As the object he made me out to be

Girls always have a secret
We were fed our own objectification at a young age
And we swallowed it whole
These lessons reached our stomachs and we stored them there
Don't wear a crop top
Or let your gut hang out
And think hard about posting a picture in a bikini
Because your stomach is your biggest secret
And once it is out
People know everything there is to know about you

For some of us
For about 25% of us[7]
Our biggest secret is rape
Our vaginas become our throats
And their manhood chokes us
And we can no longer speak
We are silenced

Or we are judged as liars, attention seekers, whores
Girls who did not make the right decisions
Girls who underestimated how easy it is for others to dehumanize us
Girls who failed to fathom the power of our objectification
Or the powerlessness of our objectification

I wonder if *shame* is synonymous with *secrecy*
I wonder if these words can be loosely translated into *women's bodies*

My life is an axle
Spinning around the word "rape"
Everything irrelevant is made relevant
Every man becomes a threat
Every bed becomes a crime scene
Every gaze becomes a mouth that says: target
And I am getting dizzy from all this spinning
So I hide in my room
Taking refuge under the sheets
But every dot on the ceiling becomes a reminder of my emptiness
Creating patterns that form into axles that spin around the word "rape"

—No escape

I get anxious when a person leaves a room
Because I'm forced to sit there and wait in the unknown
It takes me back to a moment
Where I thought it might be over
Where I thought his guilt would paralyze him
Maybe he would not come back and continue

It is this place I get stuck in
Where I lie frozen in the curve of a question mark
Wondering what will come next

I guess you could say I have control issues

I have nothing to give
But misplaced anger
So I get mad at my sister when she becomes sick
Because it forces me to realize
That I have nothing to give

— Hollow

Girls play around with some concept of objectification
It is what we are taught to do
We post pictures with an underlying caption that says:
I exist for you
It is my sole purpose in life to have you find me desirable
And it is fun and playful, like living inside of some game

But try being an actual object
Try forgetting that you have a heartbeat
Try being as frozen as a lifeless doll
It is not fun. It is not a game.
You lose everything: your real self that exists beyond the surface of
    your body
An empire that you spend your whole life building
Beyond all the skin and the social media photos
This is where your soul, heart, and passion exist
This is the source of your own unique laughter and music
This is the birthplace of all your stories and connections
This is the home of your life

But objects do not have all of this
How do you want others to perceive you?
Choose now before you post that photo with that underlying caption
Do not glorify your own objectification
Yes, the game is fun, being desired is fun
But what is the end result of never looking beyond your own surface
Do not build a path that leads to this much loss
Do not help them make you into an object
Dive deeper and fall in love with all that lives and breathes within you
Learn how much is at stake here
Protect all that is at stake here
Do not play around with this concept of your own objectification

We must shift our perception of women that are placed on pedestals
    for submitting to this concept, for being the "right" kind of girl
Glorification does not belong here; instead let compassion and
    sadness in
Feel bad for them, for your sisters
We are all being fed these messages that teach us to build a path
That points only towards Colossal Loss

— Reclaiming our Bodies

Exploring: Self-Worth

• *What messages have you received about the right and wrong way to perform girlhood? What does it mean to be a "good girl" or the "right kind of girl"?*

• *How does empowerment rooted in choice differ from this "right kind of girl" construct?*

• *If you're someone who uses social media, take some time to practice media literacy with your own feed. Explore what your intention is for posting photos and captions. Are you able to distinguish between empowered expression vs. performative posting?*

• *What is society's definition of perfection and beauty? How might these societal priorities cause body shame? How do these expectations cause harm regarding intersectional identities (race, gender, size, ability, height, etc.)?*

Nobody talks about the third survival mechanism
We always hear of fight or flight, but never freeze
I was frozen
After the *No's* and the *Please Stop's*
And the realization that I was helpless
I froze

Perhaps it was during hour two of four
It's like that movie where the patient is having surgery and they are given
    anaesthesia and their body is asleep, but they themselves are awake
Eyes shifting and a mental soundtrack playing
The only distinction between dead thing and living being

I hear the sound of my leg flopping down
As he comes back to the bed with a condom and some sickening
    newfound determination and he moves my legs apart like I am
    some rag doll
He makes himself an opening
I watched him struggle to turn me from a human to an object
And I believed him
Because I heard that flopping sound and my brain heard
"I am a doll. I am not a human."

This night is going to swallow me
And then I am going to drown
In the darkness of its throat

At what point did we stop celebrating women's power?
We used to be honoured
Our period blood worshipped
Sprinkled on fields like some sort of magic fertile pixie dust
With the belief that crops would grow faster, would grow taller
Our ability to create
Celebrated by all

At what point did this pixie dust fall into the hands of a man
Who received it as a threat?
Calling off the celebration,
"Quick" he said, "stop celebrating"
"Turn this pixie dust into shame before women learn just how high
    they can fly
Turn it to disgust before they fly so high
That us men have to look up to see them
Shielding our eyes from the sun
As the women look down upon us"

"We have to pull them down so that they have to look up at us
We have to destroy the celebration of creation
In order to not be left on the ground
In order to rise up"

— Why can't we all fly?

I like the word moonlight
What a beautiful paradox
Of darkness and light

I dove into a well of eternal depth
And it is so black and lonely down here
And my Mom is asking me questions like:
"What do you want for dinner?"
And my thoughts are so loud
And so plentiful
I am not even sure how it is possible
That all she hears is silence

My head is screaming
But my throat seems to have swallowed itself
So I guess it makes sense that the words I speak
Are only the loudest silence I've ever known

As a woman
There are two ways
To make yourself a blind spot in a man's gaze
Make yourself so big
You disappear
Make yourself so small
You disappear

Exploring: Taking Up Space

• *What are some ways that women and non-binary folk are taught to take up less space? How does this play out on a physical level (i.e., height, body size) in relationship dynamics?*

• *Western beauty standards confuse worth for weight in many harmful ways. Discuss the ways that people labeled "too thin" are treated in society. Discuss the ways that people labeled "too big" are treated in society.*

• *It is estimated that almost 30%-40% of eating disorder patients are survivors of sexual trauma.[5] Why do you think this correlation exists?*

• *Reflect on the ways that eating disorders and sexual assault may be symptoms of the same deeper issue (being the roots of objectification culture)? Though these experiences appear and express differently, what are some shared sources of suffering that may play a role in these experiences?*

Into October

I am not quite sure how a month has gone by
The days are so slow and yet they pass so quickly
I am like a passive observer watching my own life
But it is some old VCR
A home movie that keeps skipping
Quick broken glimpses that don't make much sense
My brother used to hit the television to bring it back into focus
It is much easier to watch full stories
Than random fragments that do not add up

Even when my heart is broken
Its pieces are too beautiful not to be shared

—Art

My angels said,
"Descend,
We will watch over you"
And Mother Earth wrapped her palm around me
Closing it — she said,
"It is dark,
But it is safe,
I am holding you"

And so I
Descend

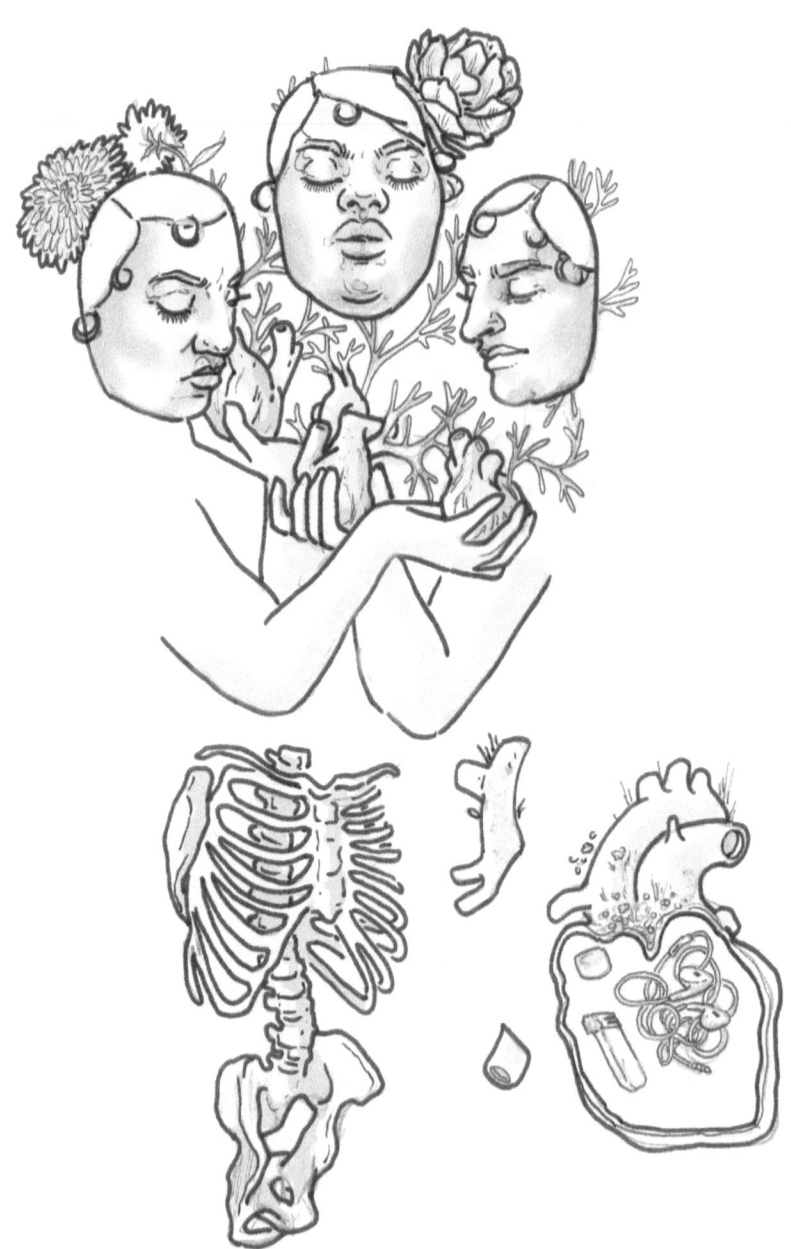

A broken heart is beautiful
Its capacity to go on existing even in pieces
The strength of its vulnerability
And its honest embrace of the pain,
The feeling

Its pieces lying shattered beside one another
Braving the brokenness until it can embrace the healing
Knowing how beautiful it will be when it all comes back together

Like the lines within a completed puzzle
The heart will one day be restored
Forevermore beautiful for its resiliency
Its history of breaking down, rebuilding

Breaking down, rebuilding

— Heart Speak

We made it all up
The isms, the wars, the standards, the politics
What we deem beautiful and what we do not
We were placed on this planet
And became pieces of a chess game
We made it all up

But we forget this
We forget to zoom out to a wider lens that captures the vastness of
the universe
To see how insignificant all these constructs are in the scheme of the
cosmos
We come and we go and we lose sight of:
What really matters?

What is true?
What has always been here?
The trees, the earth, the water, the rain
The dirt that supports us
The sky that surrounds us
This womb-like world that holds us
Always

We are all so focused on what we have created
Well, I am drowning in what we have created
And I worry what we've created will destroy us all
How are these constructions all we see underneath this vast sky that
makes it all so small in comparison?

— My soul is tired

You can be an obsessive driver
Terrified of accidents
Gripping the wheel so tightly like you are holding onto your life
Don't play music in the car
Don't speak in the car
Keep your eyes on the road
And try not to blink

But no matter what you do
No matter what precautions you take
Your safety is out of your hands
If a drunk driver swerves into your lane and hits you
Taking pieces of your life
Taking your whole life

— Repeat as many times as needed:
The rape was not my fault

I have been introduced to this other species of human
With both a heart and the capacity to harm
A people who can turn their compassion on and off like a light switch
That can quiet their conscience as if they run their minds with a remote
control

They are the kind of people you trust until they knock you off your
feet
And the confusion hits you at the same time your back hits the floor
And you're not quite sure which is the cause of all this pain

— The humanization of those that dehumanize

I spent a summer in the wilderness
And at night I walked in fear
Because you cannot reason with a cougar

Now I walk the city streets with the same fear
Because I've learned I cannot always reason with my own people
We speak the same language and yet we cannot communicate
Your desire to attack is much louder in your mind than my desperate
    words of reasoning in your ears

— Predators

Exploring: Liberation

So many aspects of our societal conditioning perpetuate binary thinking. We're often taught to think in black and white. In the following discussion questions, we'll explore ways to connect with alternative options outside of these binaries.

• *What are some ways our communities could practice rape prevention as we work towards eradicating gender-based violence? What are ways to shift the focus from "how to avoid rape" to "don't rape"?*

• *What are the binaries we've been taught around sexual expression (i.e., abstinence vs. self-objectification)? What alternative expressions of empowered sexuality exist outside of this binary? How would those expressions look and feel for you in this chapter of your life?*

• *Name some celebrities and/or role models that represent this empowered expression of sexuality, rather than perpetuating objectification. How is this person perceived by different groups of people? What are some ways that this person inspires you?*

• *What are the binaries we've been taught around relationship to food and body size (i.e., conformity vs. rebellion)? What liberating alternatives exist beyond these binaries?*

I suppose it is comforting to spin with the world
To live in synchronicity with the seasons
I was a fully blossomed flower

Bright and vibrant in the summertime
And now the leaves lose their colour
They fall off the trees and a part of me dies with them

The trees are changed but they are still trees
And the world will keep spinning until one day they regain their
     leaves
But in the meantime, let us be awed by those fall colours
And their rain-like dance of reds and yellows

— Some deaths are beautiful

Learn to hold yourself
Like a mother holds her child

I understand now how this ruins a person
How this robs a person
Every thrust into my paralyzed body was a robbery
And every day I realize how much was stolen
So no, time does not heal all

Everyday I look at a certain place within myself and I see that
What was once there is now gone
This body and this mind
From its very beginnings I have been filling it with jewels
Jewels of knowledge, love, compassion
A collection spanning a lifetime
They are all gone
My happiest memories from Before become symbols of grief
That *me* is gone
That *me* who lived like a fairy in a garden that was my enchanted world
What a beautiful image that once was
Now it looks more like a photograph beside a casket at a funeral
Some sad reminder of all the loss

Survival is killing me

I want to tell her
That I think she is the bravest girl in the world
For wearing her brokenness all over her skin

— Group sessions

You are not alone
The realization is warm soft hands wrapping around my whole heart
You are not alone
The realization is those same hands breaking my heart in two

Let's stop saying things like: protect our boys
Let's stop writing things like:
"Young men with promising futures watched as their lives fell apart"[9]
You confuse the words "victim" and "career destroyer"
Which leaves you confusing the words "rapist" and "victim"
And the contrast between opposites should be apparent
But I suppose you also confuse the words "good" and "bad"

You act like these are poor confused boys whose penises got them lost
Like some broken compass that pointed them towards rape
You have this image of them lost in a forest that is our dark society
You want to give them compassion and show them the way
Teach them their wrongs
"It is not their fault"
What a skewed image

You cannot show them the way through this mess
When they have already lit a match to shed some light on the situation
When they have already burned the entire forest down

Exploring: Victim Blaming

Discuss the following examples of victim blaming and the ways that they perpetuate patriarchal power dynamics and rape culture. Here are some examples of victim-blaming:

"Judge Robert Camp asked her several questions during that trial that he later apologized for, including: 'Why couldn't you just keep your knees together?' Camp also mistakenly referred to her as 'the accused' on several occasions during the trial and stated that, 'sometimes sex and pain go together.'"[6]

—ALBERTA SEXUAL ASSAULT CASE, 2016

"In May of 2010, Lawrence Taylor (NFL Quarterback) was charged with raping a 16-year-old runaway, believed to be forced into prostitution. Taylor pleaded guilty to having sex with 16-year-old Christina Fierro. After the jury deliberated for an hour, they ruled out that Taylor forced himself on her. L.T. received the minimum punishment of six years probation, and no jail time."[7]

• *Discuss the above examples and the ways that they perpetuate victim blaming, patriarchal power dynamics, and rape culture.*

• *Why do we teach girls and non-binary folk to avoid rape instead of teaching men not to rape? Many of us are familiar with the statistic: "1 in 4 women will be sexually assaulted"[8] but very few of us have considered how many people rape. Why do you think this is?*

• *Intersectionality is defined as, "The oppression and discrimination resulting from the overlap of an individual's various social identities."[9]*

Reflect on your own social location and the ways that you experience both privilege and oppression.

• *Discuss the ways that perpetrator empathy happens more often in privileged male populations. For instance, white cisgender men are more likely to be acquitted than Black, Indigenous, and men of colour. Why do you think this is? How can we challenge the systems and the rhetoric that uphold this inequity?*

The most beautiful part
Was when we all exhaled
And our souls came out with our breath
In the form of tears

— Survivors and solidarity

I want to jump off a bridge
But land in a pile of warm pillows
And lay there until the night comes,
When the stars find the courage to brave the black sky
And then I want to rise with the sun
Fiercely
Blindingly bright
But yes,
I want to jump off a bridge

—Dreaming in the language of nightmares

I wonder how it would feel to sit as far as the moon
How absurd it would look to see us idolizing tiny humans while we
    ignore the mountains we stand beside

What does power look like?
In all our history, how many have come and gone and worn a crown
    in-between and was it all worth it?

Our obsession with power
It makes my soul sick
We are addicted and we keep taking hits
A heroin addict feels they have found a gateway to happiness
And this, we deem a vice: a destructive substitute for real joy
At least we call it for what it is

But all of us are blind addicts filling our own holes with power, as if
    we have found a true gateway to purpose and success
Believing we are injecting importance into our veins and ignoring the costs
I think we confuse our definition of success and failure
We sacrifice love for power as if these are opposing forces
As if love itself is not power
Take off your blindfold and see that millions more have been killed by
    this obsession with influence than they have by drugs

Listen:
You will never be bigger than a mountain
No matter how huge you feel as you stand amongst those you've crushed
    with your words, your actions, your weapons

White men, oppressors, rapists, politicians
Listen:
Please,
You will never be bigger than a mountain

Music is a ship travelling across oceans
Carrying like wind across centuries, cosmos and lives
I board in my heart and set sail in my mind
I sit on the moon and breathe
I return only once I have arrived

— Sounds of Healing

Let me sink without drowning
Float to the bottom of the ocean
Weightless as a feather surrendering to gravity
Abandoning all resistance
Maybe just for a year

Let me lay here with my hands resting on my stomach
Slowly breathing in and out
My lungs filling with water, like ears filling with music
Every inhale peace
Every exhale a release of the ticking clock that lives within my mind

Let the water become me
Forgetting where my skin begins
And when every part of my body is filled with music
I will be ready to ascend

To swim against the pull of gravity and rejoin the world of the living
I know it is bright and beautiful up there
But for now I would like to sink

Let your breath be louder than your circumstances

Is there anyone who values life as deeply as the person depressed?
I expected the world to reflect the love that is in my heart
It is these expectations let down that crush my spirit
It is this idea that: life is supposed to be more
More love circling around this globe
More beauty, more compassion, more connection
More.

Perhaps a person depressed sees life more beautifully than anyone
Perhaps *depressive tendency* is mere code for: *I expect love*

— Mental "illness" is a flower

You are all so obsessed with getting to the top
You are willing to do whatever it takes to get there
Ruin lives to obtain status
Crush spirits to have people know your name
But if we all become collateral damage of your ascent, who will be
    there to know your name?
Who will you be standing over at the top of your ladder?
You will look down and see nothing
No one.

To me, the top sounds like the loneliest place in the world
To me, the top sounds much like the bottom

— *"Production for profit"*

We are experts at turning lies into truths
We play self-hatred on repeat like a broken record
And it's not long before we lose the rest of the song
Let us reverse the track
Now that we know how much we are capable of
Moulding our minds like carefully constructed sculptures
Let us turn these false truths back into lies
Let us choose better truths

— You are and always have been enough

Exploring: Mental Health

• *What are your practices for self-care? How might these practices benefit the greater good? Why do you think self-care can be falsely perceived as selfishness?*

• *Have you ever been shamed for practicing solitude or taking downtime? List off some of our culture's priorities that seem to come before mental health. What are the impacts of these priorities?*

• *What are some ways that language holds power when it comes to challenging stigma around mental health?*

• *How might these simple shifts in wording challenge the way we think of labels and identity?*

A depressed person *vs.* a person who is depressed

A happy person *vs.* a person who is happy

• *Many of us are familiar with fight and flight response, but not so much with freeze response. Why do you think this is? What are the functional and adaptive aspects of freezing out or dissociating during traumatic experiences?*

I can hear the whole world crying
It sounds like violins filling every bit of time and space
Engulfing everything that has ever come to exist
Like slow drawn-out strings so overwhelming that I am not quite sure
    if I want to run away or submerge myself completely
But the sound wraps around me like the kind of sad embrace that comes
    only with tragedy and it feels strange to tie soul-crushing grief to
    this mountainous love

But yes, it feels like returning to my mother's womb
To a place of dark haunting beauty
And my ears become open floodgates that pour music into my soul where
    every note is received urgently, gently, like a million final sunsets

I take comfort in wondering,
How much love does it take to feel this kind of heartache?

Someone please show me what true masculinity looks like
Because it hurts to accept that this toxic version is all that exists
And please don't tell me that it is about strength
Because to me, it looks more like being afraid
You think that being gentle is weak
But your fear of tenderness is so much weaker
You say things like, *"take it like a man"* and then swallow your sadness
    as if it could destroy you
And this you call *strength* instead of naming it *cowardice*

You are so terrified of what is inside you
Of the raw emotion that lives beneath your skin
Of your vulnerability
Of your own heartbeat
So if you tell me that masculinity is about strength
Then at least *"have the balls"* to admit that you are failing

— I am tired just watching
are you not tired too?

We sit in a circle and break each other with our stories one at a time
And there is so much pain
Unfathomable amounts of pain
Betrayal and loss
How much has been taken?
It is too much to grasp
And it crushes us all like we've been buried under rocks
Like we are stuck in a dark cave that blocks us from seeing the sky

And yet

None of us would be here if we had lost all hope
None of us would be here if we had forgotten the sky

Tired of having conversations with our mouths
As if our mouths are not just speaking on behalf of our souls

— Bored

Trauma itself is a global earthquake
Relentless hands that shake your world
And when the shaking stops, it has only just begun
Because you look around and become lost in the damage:
The home of your body, it has been destroyed
Your openness to trust collapsed and your sense of safety demolished
It will take us months to count the losses
Everyday you find a new reason to grieve

So ignore them when they tell you to pick up your chin
For they are choosing ignorance in the face of the aftermath
Tell them it is not so easy to move forward
When your entire world is unrecognizable

Day one:
I stared into the eyes of a stranger for two minutes
And found my own truth within her eyes:
I am scared to be seen
Scared to come out of hiding
And in my eyes she saw her own truth:
I have compassion to give and so I will give it
And I let out a breath as I chose to receive
And after two minutes of the world spinning around us,
We
Have come so far from being strangers

Day two:
I stared into the eyes of a stranger for two minutes
Silent
Stillness
Empty filled space
And what I found were the kindest eyes in the world
What I found was trust in my own heart that I had thought to be lost
And for two minutes we spoke with our eyes or our souls
And now I am unsure if we were ever really strangers

— Windows

Everything that once made me call myself beautiful
Was changed into something else
Like a dark evil twin that taunted my Light
My openness to trust became ignorant and naive
My connection to all became dumb and resentful
And I broke with the thought: *How wrong I was to love so deeply*

But in this space of beings who do love so deeply
Who find divinity in the water while celebrating the moon
I breathe as I let in this new thought:
Maybe everyone else is wrong
Maybe they are killing themselves with their denial of connection
Maybe they are walking this Earth with blindfolds and tripping over
    compassion
Maybe they are poisoning their hearts with hate
Maybe they are wrong

And this does not fix everything
Not even close
But it allows me to face the girl within me who was so happy just to
    be alive
And for the first time in a long time,
I hold her with compassion and I point my resentment somewhere else
I begin to see that this war within myself, it has been misplaced
And now I choose to stand with those who live a life of love
Infinite
Unbound
Because they are here
And I think they might be right

Because we are here and I think we are right

My father gave me power but he did not know love
My mother gave me love but she did not know power

It was the sun that taught me
The coexistence of power and love
Strength and warmth

— Fierce hearts are not a paradox

Enter November

There is some quality that bridges all the things you have done in
    your life
The lines connecting the dots that join to form a path

Everything I have ever carried out
Movement through dance
The practice of yoga
Learning tools for therapy
And the art of healing
Travelling across cultures
Seeking community
Writing these poems
Slowly,
I am beginning to see the connecting lines
The breath behind every action that has shaped my life

All I have ever wanted
Is to move beyond our words and our minds
All I have ever wanted
Is conversation that comes from our souls

—Dharma

Rain is a translator
For this universal language we all speak
Only it uses shared human experience
In place of words

—Drops together form bodies of water
Bodies together form the world

I feel as if my body is the world
My organs every mass of land
My blood flow every breathing ocean
My lungs every circulating wind

So when you came and broke my world
You broke everything that is on this Earth
North, East, South, West
Eyes, Arms, Legs, Chest
The summit of Mount Everest to the depth of Mariana Trench
My mind's eye to my grounding feet
There is no distinction between the two
All I see is brokenness

I try to focus on the light at the end of the tunnel

But I am easily distracted by the haunting fact
That I am in the depths of the tunnel in the first place

What is indestructible to you?
Value that
Because your compassion, wisdom and soul will remain with you
Long after your surface beauty has gone

Exploring: Fierce Compassion

• *In what ways have women and non-binary folk been taught that we cannot be both strong and soft? What are some messages you've received about femininity that feel disempowering? What aspects of femininity do feel empowering to you?*

• *Look at powerful women and non-binary folk throughout history. Have any off them been framed as simultaneously sweet and strong? Or have they been framed as harsh, bossy, or tyrannical?*

• *In the media, women, non-binary folk, and men are often described in the following ways:*

Women and non-binary folk	**Men**
Shrill	Direct
Bossy	Authoritative, assertive
Screaming, whining	Yelling, commanding
Emotional	Passionate, enthusiastic
Highly Strung	No-nonsense
Feisty	Tough, straightforward, lively

What other examples can you think of?

• *Reflect on the ways that you refer to women and non-binary leaders in your own interactions. In what ways might you be reinforcing oppression? In what ways do you contribute to liberation and empowerment?*

• *In 2019, my sexual assault case became one of the first in North America to conclude with restorative justice through the courts. I fought for my assailant to attend therapy, rather than proceeding to criminal trial and eventually, we met in an eight-hour circle. Why do you think we require alternatives to the punitive system? What would justice look like if it was synonymous with healing?*

❧

My wounds are not a burden
My wounds are a blessing
Without pain there can be no healing
And desperately,
This world needs healing

Selflessly
I fear for you
Draining all of your heart's resources
In loving something this broken

Selfishly
I fear for myself
Please soften the armour protecting your heart
I need you to love me while I am this broken

We are so comforted by the connection
That we find in our stories of deep isolation

— Let us be lonely together

Some days all I feel is pain
An arrow piercing through my heart

Some days that arrow is pointed skyward
And that pain feels a lot more like resilience

Perhaps we want more than a life of happiness
Perhaps what we need is a life that is full
There is so much beauty in the circle that connects
The expectations of love underlying my depression
To the celebration of life that fuels my joy

I don't want to neglect any part of that circle
Any part of myself
Any part of this life

—What I truly crave is wholeness

There is so much to learn at the bottom of the ocean
Do not be afraid to stay there and read the sand
While the rest of the world quiets

I drew my lifeline
Which formed a series of shapes and curves
That formed letters
Which formed words
That formed sentences
And then poems

— The art of my survival

Today I am a warrior
Today I am lowering the shield that has protected my heart and
    blocked my fears
What else have I lost sight of from hiding behind this barrier?
No longer can I make the whole world a blind spot

So, today my heart is a sword
With its precise point directed skywards
Carving an opening in my chest in the shape of the word "ascent"
Connecting my heart to the air I breathe before I breathe it at all
I am ready
I am restless from all this hiding
It is time to reunite my gaze with the sun
Wild and safe
Brave and warm
And I know,
For too long the sun has been waiting for this

Waiting for my homecoming

I feel it is time that I stop writing
As if I have taken up all the space I deserve
As if my voice is much too loud for my body
And for this reason
I continue to write
BIGGER and **LOUDER**
I continue to write

Nothing hurts as much as healing
Nothing is scarier than letting self-compassion in
Having to face all the things we need to heal from
Having to feel all the reasons we so desperately need to let that
    compassion in

It breaks my heart before it mends it
It abandons me in the thick of the darkness before it holds me in the light

Maybe I am focusing so much on the pain of the whole world
In order to distract from feeling my own
Maybe I am so scared of the hurt that will come
With the embrace of this compassion that is so long overdue

Is it so cowardly to pour my heart into anything but myself?
To grasp at anything that may help distract from my own self-love
    and pain?
Vanity is,
To think your worth
Is more than any other creature roaming this Earth
But vanity is also questioning,
The careful creation of your own being
To minimize my own importance
Is to doubt the creative forces that built the very ground that I walk upon

—Perhaps it is time to hold my own heart

Exploring: Powerful Conversation

- *What is the difference between power-over versus power-within?*

- *What are some examples of power that feel destructive and what are some examples of power that feel creative and life-affirming?*

- *Embodiment means being present with our bodies, needs, desires, boundaries, and emotions. Activism is all about actionably standing for certain social and political causes. What do you think it means to be an embodied activist? What could embodied activism look and feel like in your own life and in the world?*

- *Think of a time that you avoided a conversation you wanted to have in order to prevent conflict or ensure others' comfort. What was the outcome? What are some complex conversations you have had that have catalyzed growth in the long term?*

- *How might current gender constructs and binaries be detrimental to all people?*

- *Discuss the reasons that men also need feminism.*

My insides leave my body with the rivers that flow from my eyes
And I am not quite sure if afterwards I am left,
Feeling entirely empty or completely cleansed

Today the world is devastated
Today we are walking like we can no longer withstand the weight of
 gravity
Like our knees will give out and we will drop to the ground
And we will stay there for hours staring at the sky
Asking *how did this happen?*
Today this upset has shaken our world
And it feels like our souls have been violated
And we drown in a sea of the question: *how?*

But in all the tears and devastation
I feel the growth of solidarity
I hear the response to the hurt and it is: *no more*
I see people being softer with themselves and each other,
Like our hearts have all taken a beating and we are tired
Disoriented we stand in this harsh reality but perhaps here is where
 we realize:
This is not what it is supposed to be

I have never witnessed such collective sorrow
I have never felt it so deeply
But in the midst of our grief lies the call for rebirth
And it is powerful connection
It is revolutionary love
It is a heavy rainfall that makes it hard to breathe
But this is a downpour of seeds of hope and we can crumple or we
 can rise

—Election Day

Practice capturing feelings with your heart
In the same way you capture pictures with your mind

— All is within

You force-fed me hatred
And I turned it into love
How powerful that is
And I have surrounded myself with an army of warriors who do the same
Fighting back with love
We do not need that toxicity running through our veins
We have learned by experience that this world needs no more hate
We cannot begin to let our hearts resemble those who broke them in the
    first place

So breathe in healing
And breathe out gentle compassion
Keep teaching the world that love is louder
Know that if that kind of hate lived within us,
Our hearts would never have broken
Our souls would not have ached at all

Pray for more than the survival of your physical self
And do not let your Spirit die
You have faced enough loss already
Keep breathing
Inhale love
And exhale only love

The Winter Solstice comes
And I open my arms to receive one moment more of light
Pouring from the sky into each day
Droplets of comfort with this knowledge of return

In patient solitude I lie in the dark palm of Mother Earth
I spin with the seasons
I vow to ride the waves of ups and downs
To flow with the cycles of maiden, mother and crone
To celebrate the monthly cycles of my body
Of the moon
Of every passing day
Of Darkness *and* Light
And breakdowns *and* rebuilds
I let go of destinations and commit to journeys
Forget beginnings and endings,
Live moments *and* moments
One step onto this never-ending path means I am already perfect
Imperfections and all

How freeing it is to abandon resistance
To merely exist
In all the pain and bliss and sorrow and love

It is not all easy
But all is right
I am not healed
But I am forever healing

Epilogue

I HAVE ALWAYS been of the light. My sister calls me *sun goddess* (partially because she is amazing). I have always been **so** much of the light that I denied anything else within myself. I saw pain in the world and I did not want to contribute to any more of That. So until about a year ago, I denied my sadness, my right to complain and my right to cry. I minimized my trauma, invalidated my pain and became Queen of Deflection. At the hospital during my rape kit, I cried and then shut that down and said to the nurse, "Your job is really hard. Are you okay?" When I was on a yoga ashram a few summers ago, I literally Googled: *How to be sad.* I looked at myself, a privileged white, cisgender, able-bodied person, a girl favoured by her father in a middle-class family and I decided my pain should not count.

But suppression cannot coexist with healing.

And so, my descent after rape came with a crushing identity crisis, because *who was I if I was not brightening the world?* I know now how false this is. I know now that pain is immeasurable and that the comparison game becomes draining pretty quick. I know now how beautiful and humbling Grace is and so I am committing to living a life of Embrace rather than denial. I am committing to being a Whole human. I am committing to the belief that the world needs my pain just as much as it needs my joy. I know now that staying silent and denying our pain causes harm to ourselves and our communities. Whether it's a gentle whisper or a loud megaphone to the world, we deserve to speak our stories and our pain rather than suppressing them. In doing so, we teach the world to become skillful in holding space for trauma and we teach the world that this kind of violence needs to stop.

This is terrifying work, this inner-demon-exposure-type stuff: sharing this book that I initially wrote with no intention of sharing at all makes for the ultimate vulnerability hangover. But, in the depth of my depressive denial I grew desperate for external permission: for someone else to speak up or cry, to open a door for me to do the same. I hope that this book acts as a door for you — to grieve and learn and survive and love and feel life at its very fullest. This work is not easy, but I promise you it is so worth it. So many of us are standing with you.

In solidarity and infinite heart,
Marlee Liss

Resources

These resources are accurate at the time of publication.

Resources for Survivors and Allies:

Canada

Good2Talk line for post-secondary students at 1-866-925-5454, 24/7
Toronto Rape Crisis Centre at 416-597-8808 E-mail: crisis@trccmwar.ca
LGBTQ Youth Line, free at 1-800-268-9688, Text at 647-694-4275
Trans Lifeline at 1-877-330-6366
Support Service for Male Survivors of Sexual Assault at 1-888-887-0015
Canadian Resource Centre for Victims of Crime: https://crcvc.ca/

United States

National Sexual Assault Hotline operated by RAINN at 800.656.HOPE
National Child Abuse Hotline at 800.4.A.CHILD (422.2253)
National Domestic Violence Hotline at 800.799.SAFE
GLBTQ Domestic Violence Project at 800.832.1901
End Rape on Campus at endrapeoncampus.org

Worldwide

❧

RAINN (Rape, Abuse and Incest National Network) at +1 202.501.444
RAINN.org is accessible from all over the world
University of Minnesota Aurora Center advocates at 612-626-9111
International Rape Crisis Hotline Directory visit ibiblio.org/rcip/internl

*Visit www.marleeliss.com for healing resources, to learn
more about my story of restorative justice after sexual
violence or to inquire about my speaking engagements
and/or coaching programs.*

❧

Notes

These statistics are not fixed and are inconsistent across platforms.

1) Weisinger, H., Ph.D. (2011). "The Real Spirit of Anger: Psychology Today." Retrieved October 23, 2016, from www.psychologytoday. com /blog/thicken-your-skin/201105/the-real-spirit-anger

2) Plataforma SINC. (2010, June 1). "What happens when we get angry?" ScienceDaily. Retrieved October 23, 2016 from www.sciencedaily. com /releases/2010/05/100531082603.htm

3) P. (2015). "What is Objectification: GoodTherapy.org." Therapy Blog. Retrieved October 23, 2016, from www.goodtherapy.org/blog /psychpedia/definition-of-objectification

4) Maltz, W. (2001). *The sexual healing journey: A guide for survivors of sexual abuse.* Quill.

5) A. (2007). "Eating Disorders: After Silence." Retrieved October 23, 2016, from www.aftersilence.org/eating-disorders.php

6) Fletcher, R. (2016). "'Knees together' judge should lose job, judicial committee recommends." Retrieved January 01, 2017, from www.cbc.

7) "15 Athletes Who Got Away With Crimes." (2015). Retrieved January 01, 2017, from www.thesportster.com/entertainment/15-athletes -who-got-away-with-crimes/

8) Sexual Assault Statistics in Canada. (n.d.). Retrieved January 01, 2017, from www.sexassault.ca/statistics.htm

9) Intersectionality. (n.d.). Retrieved January 01, 2017, from www .dictionary.com/browse/intersectionality

❧

About the Author

MARLEE LISS is a restorative justice advocate, award-winning speaker, and embodiment coach. She is also a Jewish, lesbian feminist and trailblazer. Marlee made history in the justice system when her sexual assault case became the first in North America to conclude with restorative justice through the courts. This means that she fought for her assailant to go to therapy instead of proceeding to criminal trial and eventually, they met in a transformative eight-hour circle. Since then, Marlee has shared her story worldwide, being featured on major media platforms such as *Forbes, Huff Post, Buzzfeed, The Mel*

Robbins Show, and more. Additionally, with a background in anti-oppressive social work, eating disorder prevention, trauma-informed yoga and somatic sex education, Marlee has coached hundreds of women and non-binary folk worldwide in reclaiming sensuality and embodied empowerment, especially after sexual trauma, disordered eating, and relationship abuse.

A renowned speaker, Marlee won first place at the international Speaker Slam competition on Forgiveness and has delivered presentations for the US Military Sexual Assault Response Team, on an elite panel for the National Action Plan to End Gender-Based Violence, at Fordham School of Law, University of Toronto, the National Restorative Justice Symposium, and more. Additionally, she is the creator of The Sensual Revolution Podcast and her signature coaching programs, which have positively impacted many.

Learn more about Marlee's work at www.marleeliss.com and follow her journey on social media at @marleeliss.

❧